Counting
CALICO

Phyllis Limbacher Tildes

Scholastic Inc.
New York   Toronto   London   Auckland   Sydney

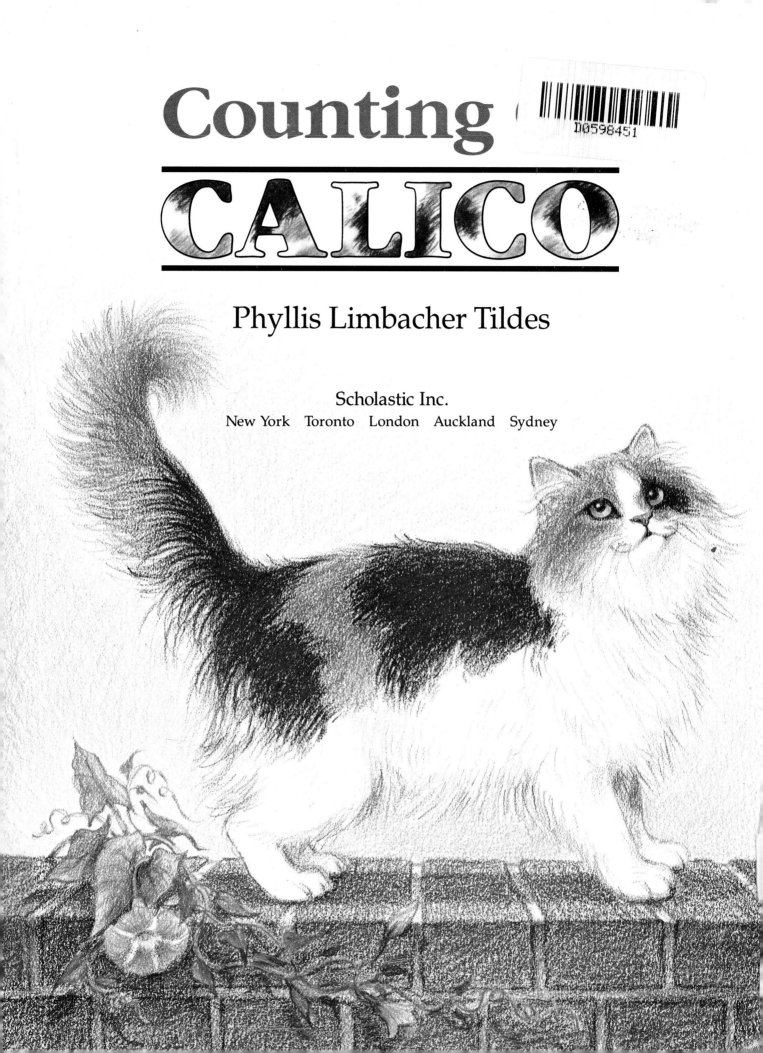

In loving memory of my parents,
Olga and Philip Limbacher

ISBN 0-590-74563-8

Copyright © 1995 by Phyllis Limbacher Tildes.
All rights reserved. Published by Scholastic Inc.,
555 Broadway, New York, NY 10012, by arrangement with
Charlesbridge Publishing.

12 11 10 9 8 7 6 5 4 3 2   6 7 8 9/9 0 1/0

Printed in the U.S.A.   14

First Scholastic printing, February 1996

Hello, my name is Willy Whiskers.
I'm the Squeaker of the House.
Let me show you how to
count on a cat.

I know a
calico cat.
We can count
on her.

She has...

1 tail

A cat uses its tail for balance, but you can use the tail to tell how a cat is feeling. A raised tail means a cat is happy. A twitching tail means a cat is angry or is getting ready to pounce. It's hard to figure out a Manx cat — it has no tail at all!

2 big eyes

Many cats have green or yellow eyes, but the eyes of Siamese and Persian cats are blue. When cats hunt at night, their eyes seem to glow in the dark. Their pupils open wide in dim light. They can see eight times better at night than people can. Even so, cats can see only what is in front of them. To watch a mouse running across the floor, or the path of a swinging string, a cat has to turn its entire head.

3 black spots

Calico cats have only spots of black fur. Cats that are all black scare some people. Why? Long ago, people believed that when a black cat stared into a witch's fire it made the witch's magic work! People also believed that you would have bad luck if a black cat crossed your path. Of course, any cat can be bad luck to a mouse or bird.

4 legs

Cats' legs are very strong and flexible. They are perfect for jumping and running. How high can you jump? A cat can jump five times its own height! Cats can run faster than mice. Unless a mouse runs into a nearby hole, it may be caught and played with like this yarn.

5 paw pads

Can you walk as silently as a cat? A cat can pull in its claws and sneak up on its soft paw pads. These pads also cushion the landing when a cat jumps down from a high place.

Cat paws may keep moving even when the cat is resting! Cats open and close their paws while pushing with one foot then the other in a movement called kneading. This means they are content or happy and probably purring.

6 orange spots

Cats come in many colors and patterns. A calico cat is a white female with orange and black spots. The word *calico* comes from the name of a colorful cloth made in the city of Calcutta, India. If you find a male calico, report it to the veterinarian. That rare cat will make you famous!

7 newborn kittens

Kittens are born quite helpless, but they know
how to cry and how to use their sense of smell to
find where to drink their mother's warm milk.
Their eyes will not open for about ten days, and
their mother has to wash, feed, protect, and
hide them in a dark place. When they are
bigger, they will watch what she does
to learn about the world.

8 bowls of food

When kittens are about one month old, it is time for them to learn to eat food. They don't know what to do. They watch their mother and are curious about the delicious smells. Before long, they stick their noses in their food and, oh, what a mess! Did you ever sit in your bowl when you were learning to eat?

Calico

9 lives

Cats don't really have nine lives, but they do seem to survive danger magically. A falling cat turns in mid-air to land on its feet. Cats can squeeze into and out of very small spaces. A fast and clever cat could live 20 years. The oldest cat on record was 34 years old!

See that Maine Coon Cat in the top corner? That's the kittens' daddy.

10 front claws

Watch out for cats' claws!
Claws are used for
hunting, climbing trees,
or shredding furniture.
A cat scratches to remove
the outer layer of the claw
and make a sharp new tip.
Each claw is bent like a
fishhook. That shape
makes it easy to climb
up a tree but hard to
climb down.

11 birds to watch

Cats will spend hours watching birds at a feeder. Even watching through a window, a cat will tense its muscles as though it is getting ready to pounce. The cat's natural instincts to hunt are so strong that some cat owners hang a bell on their cat's collar to warn animals that a cat is coming.

12 moths to catch

Moths are attracted to light and cats are attracted to fluttering wings. A moth is fun to catch and makes a tasty midnight snack for a cat. What's your favorite snack?

13 paper bags

There's an old saying, don't let the cat out of the bag! It means don't tell a secret. It is no secret that cats like to climb in and out of grocery bags and boxes. This is a great place for kittens to play. They can't resist exploring dark places. Do you have a favorite hiding place?

14 ears to wash

Can you wiggle your ears? Cats can move their ears around to hear the slightest sound. They turn their ears back and flatten them down when they are frightened or angry. Most of the time, a cat's ears are upright and ready for washing. A cat's tongue is covered with hundreds of rough bumps that comb dirt, loose hairs, or food out of its fur.

15 ways to sleep

 Kittens are never too old for a cat nap. When they sleep, they twist themselves into odd positions. A cat can even curl its back into a half circle. Cats are one of the "sleeping-est" mammals. They sleep as many as 16 hours a day!

16 front teeth

Even a kitten has sharp little baby teeth. When it grows up it will have 30 teeth in all! The 16 front teeth are easy to see while the cat is yawning. How many teeth do you have?

17 whiskers

Cat whiskers are very sensitive "feelers." They help cats feel their way around in the dark and through tight spaces. The cat marks its belongings with scent from glands behind its whiskers. When a cat rubs its face against a person or furniture it may be showing affection or it may be saying, "You belong to me."

18 toys

Cats pretend they are hunting when they play. They can't resist a rolling, spinning, or swinging toy. Even a crumpled up piece of paper is worth a sniff and a poke. Toys are as important to cats as they are to children.

19 goldfish

Most cats do not like to get wet. Unlike tigers and the little Turkish Van cat, who jump right into water, house cats will only put a paw in to try flipping out a fish. This kitten will have to learn that this is a game no one is allowed to play. Please tell that kitten to get down from there!

20 wet paw prints

Twenty wet paw prints lead right to me — I'll hide in my mousehole, where kittens can't see.